JEFF GORDON

TRIUMPH

Author:
Woody Cain

Photography:
The Charlotte Observer

Editor:
Constance Holloway

Design Team:
Larry Preslar
Beth Epperly
Andrea Ross

This book is a joint production of Triumph Books and the New Ventures Division of Knight Publishing Co.

This book is not sponsored, authorized or endorsed by or otherwise affiliated with NASCAR or any person featured within this book. This is not an official publication.

This book is available in quantity at special discounts for your group or organization. For further information, contact:

Triumph Books
601 South LaSalle Street, Suite 500
Chicago, Illinois 60605
(312) 939-3330
Fax (312) 663-3557

Printed in the United States of America

ISBN 1-57243-523-2

Woody Cain is a journalist living in Concord, North Carolina with his wife, Sandy. A graduate of Appalachian State University, he has covered motorsports for radio, television, and print since 1987. Cain is host of the live call-in television program *Let's Talk Racing*, and play-by-play announcer for the televised *Around the Track* racing productions and specials.

Other professional credits include work as a general reporter and editor for daily, weekly, and monthly publications, as well as radio news/sports director at WEGO-AM in Concord and WABZ-FM in Albemarle, North Carolina. Cain currently works as editor of, The Charlotte Observer's University City Magazine in Charlotte, North Carolina.

JEFF GORDON stats

Cars:

No. 24 Dupont Chevy (Winston Cup), No. 24 Pepsi Chevy (Busch Grand National)

Major Wins: 58

- Won Coca-Cola 600 at Charlotte ('94, '97, '98)
- At age 25, became the youngest driver to win the Daytona 500 ('97, '99)
- Winner, inaugural Brickyard 400 ('94, '98, '01)
- Winner, Busch Clash ('94, '97)
- Winner, Southern 500 ('95, '96, '97, '98)
- Winner, The Winston ('95, '97, '01)

Earnings:

$47 million (Winston Cup)

Poles:

41

Top 5 Finishes:

151

Top 10 Finishes:

199

Championships:

- Winston Cup Rookie of the Year ('93)
- Winston Cup Championship ('95, '97, '98, '01)
- Driver-of-the-Year award ('97, '98)

Teams:

Rick Hendrick Motorsports

Sponsors:

Dupont, Pepsi, Chevy, Quaker State, GMAC, Automotive Finish, Fritos

Fun Facts:

At age 24, Gordon was second-youngest driver to win the Winston Cup Championship. Set Busch Grand National record with 11 poles. Won all three segments of the Winston Select all-star race at Charlotte in 1995. Two-time winner of the Winston Million. Won four consecutive races—July '98 to late August—and tied modern-era record. Tied modern-era record with 13 wins in a season. Won record-breaking six consecutive road course events ('97-'00).

TABLE OF CONTENTS

THE KID
with a moustache

Before Jeff Gordon burst onto the scene in 1993, accepted wisdom said stock car drivers were born and raised under the shade trees of the South, where they worked on cars then took them to their local short track on Saturday nights.

The better ones progressed through the ranks over the years with a lot of grease and hard luck along the way.

The best of those, if they were fortunate enough to convince some-one—anyone—to give them a shot at the big time, went racing for NASCAR's Winston Cup.

Gordon seemed to tilt the status quo on its ear.

Since he had come up through the Midget and Sprint Car ranks, many longtime NASCAR fans had never heard of Jeff Gordon. Some even scoffed at his chances for suc-

cess when he made the move to stock cars in 1991.

Despite Gordon's array of accomplishments, NASCAR insiders privately expressed amusement in fall 1990 when he visited Charlotte (now Lowe's) Motor Speedway for an open practice session to test a Grand National car.

"That absolutely is the youngest kid I've ever seen with a moustache," said one.

Born August 4, 1971 in Vallejo, California, and raised in Pittsboro, Indiana, Gordon began his racing career at five years old when his stepfather, John Bickford, put him in a Quarter Midget car after his moth-er worried BMX bicycle racing might be too dangerous. He flipped the car five times practicing for his first organized race but came back to set the fastest qualifying time.

> *"That absolutely is the youngest kid I've ever seen with a moustache," said one.*

Winning soon became a way of life. Later, his family moved to Indiana when California age restrictions started limiting where he could race. By age 19, he was the youngest champion ever in the U.S. Auto Club's Midget series.

By the time he was 20, he had twice been named to the All-American Team by the American Racing Writers and Broadcasters Association, joining such legends as Dale Earnhardt, Harry Gant, Michael Andretti, and Rick Mears.

Gordon paid his dues by winning four national go-kart class championships, Quarter-Midget national championships in 1979 and '81, a U.S. Auto Club Midget championship in 1990, and the 1991 USAC Silver Crown championship trophy. He won more than 500 short track events, many of them televised on ESPN's *Saturday Night Thunder* series, bringing him national popularity.

When he was granted his USAC racing license on his 16 birthday, Gordon became the youngest-ever driver on that circuit, and he posted 22 wins, 21 poles, 55 top-five finishes, and 66 top-10 finishes over 93 starts in four divisions.

Opting for a NASCAR career over open-wheel Indy Car racing, Gordon came south in 1991 to drive Fords for team owner Bill Davis on the Grand National tour. He didn't win that first season, but his diamond-in-the-rough talent was apparent. He finished second three times and third once. He had five top-five and 10 top-10 finishes, won one pole position and two outside poles, and wound up 11th overall in the point standings, earning Rookie-of-the-Year honors.

In a 300-miler at Atlanta Motor Speedway in March 1992, Gordon drove to his first NASCAR checkered flag.

"The last lap, I almost lost the race because I was so choked up all the way around," said Gordon.

He had no way of knowing it at the time, but his showing that day was to lead to a dramatic turn in his career. Gordon added two more victories that season, taking both 300-milers at Charlotte Motor Speedway from the pole. Overall, he won 11 poles, a Grand National single-season record.

In the first Charlotte win in May, Gordon pulled a daring pass for the lead that would have made any stock car racing veteran proud and charged to a victory in the Champion 300. The triumph was worth a NASCAR Grand National Series record purse of $115,125 for Gordon, 20, and the Bill Davis team. It undoubtedly meant an even bigger marketing bonanza for Ford, which was winless in 33 Grand National races at Charlotte until Gordon flashed under the checkered flag that day.

A sheet-metal-scrubbing pass of veteran Dick Trickle in Turn 4 on the 163rd of the race's 200 laps was the key and Gordon steadily pulled away from there. It was a risky three-cars-wide maneuver, as the lapped Oldsmobile of Phil Parsons also was involved.

"I had a lot of close calls out there," said Gordon. "That pass was one of them. We were rubbing, but rubbing is racing."

There seemed no doubt Gordon would graduate to the Winston Cup Series in 1993 with Davis and Ford, which had championed his entry to NASCAR. However, at a race in Nazareth, Pennsylvania, word leaked that Gordon had signed to join Hendrick Motorsports, a Chevrolet operation, in '93. Through an incredible oversight, Ford officials hadn't protected the company in the phenom's contract.

Controversy ensued. Ford threatened to sue but never did, and Gordon moved to Charlotte to join team owner Rick Hendrick. The determination of Hendrick to hire Jeff Gordon as a driver was inspired that cold spring Saturday when the youngster was en route to victory in the Atlanta 300-miler.

"I was on my way to a VIP suite in Turn 1 and the cars were going by right under us," recalled Hendrick. "This one guy had his car so sideways in the corner that smoke was boiling from the rear tires every lap.

"I told a friend that was with me, 'Just watch. In a lap or two that

guy's going to bust his fanny. No one can drive a car that's running that loose for long.'

"But this guy did. . . . He drove it to victory lane. Of course, it was Jeff Gordon.

"I said to myself right then that I wanted a fellow with the ability to handle a car like that driving for me."

up to CUP

Jeff Gordon made his NASCAR Winston Cup Series debut in the 1992 season finale, the final race of Richard Petty's driving career.

Gordon broke in to Winston Cup in '93 more sensationally than even Hendrick could have imagined. He won a 125-mile qualifying race at Daytona International Speedway, experiencing a fateful introduction in victory lane. He then dogged Dale Earnhardt's bumper for much of the Daytona 500 before Dale Jarrett passed them both on the last lap. Gordon wound up fifth in the 500, an auspicious debut.

To his disappointment, Gordon didn't win a regular-season race in his first year, but he was runner-up twice, had five other top-five finishes, and four other top 10s en route to $765,168 in winnings, 14th place in the points standings, and the Rookie-of-the-Year title.

There was no doubt 1994 would be a sensational season for Gordon, young enough to be the son of many of his rivals. It exceeded expectations.

First came victory in February's Busch Clash, a race at Daytona matching the previous season's pole winners. Finally, amidst deep drama, came a regular-season win.

Through the Coca-Cola 600 at Charlotte in May, Rusty Wallace and Geoff Bodine dueled for the lead, with Gordon lurking a bit behind in his No. 24 Chevy with the brilliant, multicolored paint scheme.

With a record crowd watching the first nighttime finish of the classic, Bodine and Wallace pitted for four tires and fuel. Then, Gordon came onto pit road and was out in a flash. Crew chief Ray Evernham had called for only right side tires, a brilliant decision that put Gordon in the lead. He never gave it up.

"That pit stop won the race for us," said Gordon afterward. "It was a great call."

> *Gordon broke in to Winston Cup in '93 more sensationally than even Hendrick could have imagined.*

"Ray and I talk a lot about the things we want to do in racing, and one of them was that we didn't want to sneak up on our first win—get it because someone wrecked or got a yellow flag at the wrong time. We wanted to go out there and beat them on the race track or in the pits. We wanted to do it the way it is supposed to be done."

As huge as the Charlotte triumph was for Gordon and his team, a larger one awaited on August 6.

For more than eight decades, the only auto race held at Indianapolis Motor Speedway was the Indianapolis 500. Eventually, NASCAR's explosion in popularity made it inevitable that a Winston Cup event would be held at the 2.5-mile track. The Brickyard 400 was born.

"Everyone was excited to be racing at Indy, me especially since I'd grown up nearby," said Gordon. "I was really hopeful of running well.

"The first lap in practice I knew we had a great car. I felt we had a shot at the pole, but I slipped and we wound up third, and I was pretty happy with that. In practice the next day, there wasn't anybody I couldn't run down."

During the race, attended by a NASCAR record crowd estimated at 300,000, Gordon battled with Geoff Bodine for the lead until Bodine was sidelined by a bumping incident with his brother, Brett. Then, Ernie Irvan, moving up from

the middle of the pack, engaged Gordon in a thrilling duel until Irvan cut a tire with five laps to go. Gordon then held Brett Bodine at bay to become the first Brickyard 400 winner, assuring a prominent place in motorsports history.

"That inaugural race was bigger than life as far as I'm concerned," said Gordon, who won a NASCAR-record $613,000. "I didn't know how much the race paid until the next day when I saw the paper.

"The money means nothing to me. . . . I'm sure I'll enjoy it, but the main thing to any guy in the facility driving a race car that day is that he wanted to win the race, no matter what.

"There's only going to be one guy to win the first one, take that checkered flag, and drive into victory lane to enjoy that excitement. We were that team and I was that guy. There wasn't anybody in the world that I'd have traded places with at that moment.

"I guess if you look at the race in a certain way, it looked like it was fixed, me being from Indiana and all. But it really wasn't. NASCAR didn't give us any more breaks than anybody else."

3

A CHAMPION *emerges*

By April 1995, Gordon was being taken seriously as a threat for the Winston Cup championship. He won the pole for the First Union 400 at North Wilkesboro Speedway, his fourth pole in the first seven races. And he had already won three of the previous six races.

An all-Ford front row of Brett Bodine and Derrike Cope seemed likely at the five-eighths-mile track until Gordon took his Monte Carlo on the track 43rd among 45 qualifiers. He edged Bodine as rivals shook their heads and muttered about "the Wonder Boy doing it to us again."

In four previous races at North Wilkesboro, Gordon had qualified seventh, 16th, 12th, and 12th. Bodine's bid in a Thunderbird fielded by local hero Junior Johnson brought a roar from several thousand fans hoping to see his team break out of a slump.

Gordon, told he might have a shot at a record for poles in a season, smiled and said, "I don't think about records and stuff. . . . Really, I can't believe this is happening."

The nicknames were inevitable for Jeff Gordon, the NASCAR Winston Cup Series racing phenom.

"Wonder Kid" and "Wonder Boy" surfaced at North Wilkesboro. The first nickname seemed to indicate a feeling of admiration and warmth. The latter carries a bit sharper connotation.

"I know it's difficult to see a 23-year-old like me come in and start winning," Gordon said. "It would be difficult for me, too, if I was getting beat by someone younger.

"I know there's nothing personal in how the other drivers and teams feel about me."

Gordon proved to be talented and mature beyond his years, especially in how he handled the most

The nicknames "Wonder Kid" and "Wonder Boy" surfaced at North Wilkesboro.

sensational start ever for a NASCAR competitor so young.

While proud of what he and the Chevrolet team owned by Charlottean Rick Hendrick had accomplished—they also won the Coca-Cola 600 and Brickyard 400 "majors" in 1994—Gordon took a common-sense approach to his success.

"I think people realize I just go out there and try to keep my job like everyone else," he said. "Nobody is going to come up to me and say, 'Hey, I don't like you because you're winning all the races.' I don't see that. It might be out there, but no one has made it evident to me personally."

His learning curve certainly seemed shorter than most young drivers', but Gordon said he had already absorbed some key points.

"It's a lot more than which way to turn the steering wheel and how hard to push the gas pedal," he said. "It's where you have patience, where you're aggressive. Also how to keep cool and keeping my head straight no matter what happens."

The North Wilkesboro pole seemed to set discussion of a possible championship run afire.

"If we do find ourselves in the battle, we'll deal with it then," Gordon said. "If this is the year, well, we're certainly not thinking that way. When I won the championship in USAC and Midget racing, I didn't think those were the years, either. I just found myself in the lead all of a sudden and, boom, we won the championships. Dale Earnhardt knows every year he's going for a championship. We don't."

There was also an obvious growing rivalry with Earnhardt, the seven-time champion who for years had been Chevy's ace, carrying nicknames of his own like "The Intimidator," a tribute to his aggressive driving style.

"I've never been in a situation with Earnhardt where I thought anything [contact between their race cars] was deliberate," Gordon said. "This is another place where he comes to the front, no matter what. I don't know whether he was just

having fun or getting crazy. I expect some more of that. I hope he expects some, too.

"It's not like we're battling to see who is boss. I think I'm being put to the test, and I want to pass the test. If I'm going to be graded, I want an A. Earnhardt does that to a lot of guys. He plays with them, whether it be on the track or off it. Sometimes I don't know how to take him, but I still enjoy it."

Gordon didn't win that North Wilkesboro race. He finished second to Earnhardt and the rivalry became the buzz of the sport.

In May, Gordon added to his growing legend by winning The Winston Select all-star race, leading all three segments of the wreck-marred event at Charlotte. In a dominating performance, Gordon won $300,000.

In July he had all the right moves in winning a final-lap sprint in the Pepsi 400 at Daytona International Speedway.

The win was the fourth of the Winston Cup season for Gordon,

but his first in a series championship event at Daytona's 2.5-mile track.

"It's just getting more and more incredible," Gordon said.

By August, when the series headed back to Indy, Gordon was all the rage. Terry Labonte was at a podium during a Brickyard 400 sponsor luncheon, accepting a few questions from the motorsports media.

"What speed will it take to win the pole?" Labonte was asked.

He turned to his young Hendrick Motorsports teammate and asked, "How fast are you going to run?"

Gordon's response was a laugh, shared by everyone else in the hospitality tent at Indianapolis Motor Speedway.

Earnhardt soon injected the first bit of gamesmanship into the chase for the championship. Gordon's crew chief, Ray Evernham, had made a public request that the nickname pinned on his 24-year-old driver not be used anymore. There was no compliance from Earnhardt.

"'Wonder Boy' is out there showing no fear," Earnhardt said.

"He's going wide open, so we've got to go out there and work hard, too. That makes us better to have competition like that, someone to push us to the next plateau or limit or whatever."

During the Hurricane Opal-spawned rainy days leading up to the UAW-GM Quality 500 at Charlotte in October, Evernham made his pitch again.

"Jeff Gordon deserves respect," Evernham said. "And he shouldn't be called Wonder Boy.'"

The minute Evernham said it, you could almost hear Dale Earnhardt cackling in mischievous delight.

As the season wound down, Gordon's confidence grew and he said he felt destined to win.

"The big guy upstairs, he's going to make sure we got to work for it," Gordon said. "I don't think he's going to take it away from us, but I honestly feel he's going to make it real close."

Gordon wanted to finish the season with a flourish and win at

Atlanta to wrap up the title and close the season with an emphatic stamp, but defending-series champion Earnhardt scored a dominating victory in the NAPA 500. It wasn't enough to overtake Gordon for the NASCAR Winston Cup championship, however, worth a minimum of $1.3 million.

Gordon actually clinched a first title for himself and Hendrick Motorsports when he led the 61st of the race's 328 laps for five bonus points.

"We know Earnhardt isn't going away just because we won this year," Gordon said.

1995 Final Winston Cup Standings

1. Jeff Gordon	4,614
2. Dale Earnhardt	4,580
3. Sterling Marlin	4,361
4. Mark Martin	4,320
5. Rusty Wallace	4,240
6. Terry Labonte	4,146
7. Ted Musgrave	3,949
8. Bill Elliott	3,746
9. Ricky Rudd	3,734
10. Bobby Labonte	3,718

fierce COMPETITOR

4

The next year brought one of the closest championship finishes in the history of the Winston Cup Series.

In 1996 Gordon entered the NASCAR Winston Cup Series racing season with the goal of winning the circuit's championship.

"Our goals are different than they were last year," he said. "In '95 we went into the season just hoping to finish in the top five in the point standings. This time we go in aiming for the championship."

Gordon won 10 races and had a 110-point lead over teammate Terry Labonte with four races left. Labonte won his second championship by winning at Charlotte and finishing third at Rockingham and Phoenix (while driving with a broken finger suffered in a practice crash), then driving to a fifth-place finish in the season finale at Atlanta. Labonte edged Gordon by 37 points for the title.

The next year brought one of the closest championship finishes in

the history of the Winston Cup Series. Gordon won the season-opening Daytona 500, then made it two in a row with a win the following week at Rockingham.

At Bristol in April 1997, Gordon muscled his Chevrolet past short track ace Rusty Wallace's Ford in the final turn to win the Food City 500, putting an exciting climax on a metal-mashing race. Gordon chased Wallace down during a heart-stopping, 50-lap green flag fight to the finish that followed a 450-lap demolition derby—the race's 20 caution flags tied a modern NASCAR record at the time.

After fending off Terry Labonte's effort to pass him for second, Gordon closed on Wallace's rear bumper down the backstretch on the final lap and the cars made contact in the final set of turns.

Gordon's short-track-style tap

pushed Wallace just high enough for Gordon to dive inside and get to the finish line first by less than a half-second.

"It's every man for himself at Bristol, so I really didn't know what was going to happen on that last lap," Gordon said after winning his third-straight spring race at Bristol and his third victory of the '97 season. "We were battling Rusty or he was battling us all day long. We figured it was going to come down between the two of us.

"Once I got on his bumper, I just tried to put as much heat on him as I could. . . . I came off [Turn] 2 on the white-flag lap and got a great run. I kind of pushed Rusty all the way down the back straight.

As we got into [Turn] 3, he got a little bit loose and we touched a little bit. A hole opened up and I went for it.

"I've seen things like that hap-

pen many times here at Bristol, but I was never part of them. It was definitely the most exciting finish I think I've ever had in my career.'"

"I wasn't surprised he touched me," Wallace said. "I would have probably done the same thing if I had gotten that close going for the checkered [flag]. Here at Bristol, you can touch a little bit and that will do."

Gordon made it two straight wins again at Martinsville the next week, surviving a 360-degree spin to score a dominating victory in the Goody's 500. Gordon's victory at Martinsville the year before had been his first at the .526-mile track.

"I have a lot of confidence at some race tracks, and this is starting to be one of them," he said.

In September 1997, one lap away from $1 million, Jeff Gordon looked in his mirror and saw Jeff Burton coming. In the week before the Southern 500 at Darlington

Raceway, Gordon told everybody what would happen if he found himself in that situation.

"I said if it came down to the last lap, I was going to do whatever it took to win it," Gordon said.

What it took was a fender-banging battle down the front stretch under the white flag and into the first turn of the final lap, with Gordon edging out Burton to become the second driver to win the "Winston Million" bonus.

Gordon needed to win the Southern 500 to go with his wins at Daytona and Charlotte that season to claim the Winston Million, a bonus for winning any three of the so-called "Big Four" races on the NASCAR Winston Cup circuit.

He won it the hard way.

With a million dollars' worth of help from his pit crew, the "Rainbow Warriors," Gordon won it with a car that was not good enough to

win it. He won it despite slamming into the wall; won it despite falling far behind at one point; won it by putting a fender into Jeff Burton on the last lap when that was the only way he could keep Burton from passing him for the win. Four hours of racing turned into an epic of banging and slamming and narrow escapes, and a frantic hunt for something that would make the car go faster would keep it up front with Dale Jarrett and Bill Elliott and Burton.

"The money is always an afterthought to me," Gordon said. "When there's a big prize up there, a lot of times it's big dollars. But I don't think of it like I am going for all this money. To me, that's just a bigger trophy."

The most significant thing about the victory wasn't the million bucks. It was that Gordon, at age 26, won the Southern 500, the most demanding test in stock car racing,

for the third year in a row.

Some criticized Gordon for "cutting down" on Burton in their thundering, grinding stretch run.

But when asked if he would be mad had the situation been reversed, Gordon said, "I would've expected it. I would probably have said, 'Man, he ran me down low,' which I did, but when I got home and thought about it, I would say I would've done the same thing.

"I can't imagine it getting any more exciting. I've said all week if it came down to the last lap and I was in the top two or three, watch out, there's a guy going for a million bucks and three Southern 500s in a row. The gloves are off at that point.

"I'm sure he's not happy. But I wouldn't have taken him out to win the race. He could've wrecked me and probably won, but he didn't and I respect that."

Burton was mad enough to try

"to put him in the wall and I just missed him." But then Burton didn't blame Gordon. "He did what he had to do to win the race," Burton said.

STRETCH run

Entering the last five races of 1997, Gordon led Mark Martin by 135 points and Dale Jarrett by 222. Jarrett won at Charlotte and Martin was fourth, but Gordon finished fifth.

At Talladega the next week a 23-car pile-up ensued when Gordon blew a tire and slashed across the track, starting a chain reaction that damaged every car in the top five in points. Terry Labonte won and Gordon finished 35th. Jarrett wound up 21st and Martin come home 30th. Both missed a chance to make up ground in the points battle.

From there it was on to Rockingham where Bobby Hamilton won in a race held on Monday after rain postponed the event a day earlier. Jarrett finished second and Martin sixth, but Gordon held his pursuers at bay with a fourth-place finish. Jarrett won his seventh race of the year the next week at

Phoenix and Martin drove to sixth, but Gordon battled back to 17th after a late flat tire forced him to pit under green. Jarrett and Martin were within 100 points with one race left: Atlanta.

Gordon started off by spinning into Hamilton on pit road during practice, forcing the 24 team to a backup car. Bobby Labonte won the race while Jarrett and Martin came in second and third. Gordon fought his way to 17th again—enough to win the championship by just 14 over Jarrett and 29 over Martin— the closest battle among three drivers for the title in series history. It also represented the third straight title for Hendrick Motorsports. The $1.5 million championship check and other season-ending awards pushed Gordon's 1997 winnings close to $6 million, erasing the single-season record of $4.3 million he set in win-

> *"It's hard to put into perspective what I have accomplished. I didn't honestly believe everything was going to take place."*

ning the 1995 crown.

"I really don't try to set numbers and say I have to win this many races or this many championships to accomplish everything," Gordon said. "All my life I have been brought up to win the Daytona 500, to win the Indianapolis 500, to be the greatest race car driver I can be, and to race with some of the greats.

"I didn't honestly believe that was going to happen, and even now that I'm living it, I have to say I never dreamed it would actually come true."

By now, Gordon had appeared in a commercial with Shaquille O'Neal. He'd done the TV talk thing with David Letterman and Jay Leno. He was interviewed by Cindy Crawford, and was on *People* magazine's list of the "50 most beautiful people." He signed a deal with the William Morris Agency, joining Crawford, Bruce Willis, Bill Cosby, and John Travolta on that agency's list of clients.

"I'm just so thrilled to be where I am," Gordon said, "to be able to compete at the Winston Cup level. I want to be able to drive the race car and be competitive for a long time, whether that's 10 or 20 years.

"I've already accomplished so much and I'm so satisfied with where my career is and what I've accomplished. I don't know how it gets much better than this. The rest from here is just icing on the cake, but that doesn't stop us from setting goals each year to try to win another championship and try to win more races.

"It's so much different when you're experiencing it than when you're looking at it happen to somebody else from the outside," Gordon added. "It's hard to put into perspective what I have accomplished. I didn't honestly believe everything was going to take place. Now that I am living it, even I never actually dreamed it would all come

true. When you're living it, you are so focused on that moment and on what the next step is, you really can't enjoy it until you are somewhere down the road and you can look back on it."

1997 Final Winston Cup
Standings (Top 10)

1. Jeff Gordon		4,710
2. Dale Jarrett		4,696
3. Mark Martin		4,681
4. Jeff Burton		4,285
5. Dale Earnhardt		4,216
6. Terry Labonte		4,177
7. Bobby Labonte		4,101
8. Bill Elliott		3,836
9. Rusty Wallace		3,598
10. Ken Schrader		3,576

NASCAR's 50th anniversary season kicked off in 1998 with Dale Earnhardt's first-ever Daytona 500 win. Earnhardt dominated a 125-mile qualifying race before the 500 and Gordon won an International Race

of Champions event leading up to NASCAR's "Super Bowl".

Earnhardt ended two decades of frustration in the 500, scoring a heart-pounding victory to stop the two most maddening streaks of his racing career. Earnhardt had won 30 races at the 2.5-mile mother church of stock car racing, but never Winston Cup racing's biggest event, the season-opening 500. He also had gone 59 races, almost two full seasons, without winning anywhere. Both streaks were washed away in his 20th start in a race he had led four times before with 10 laps to go, only to lose in heartrending fashion.

Earnhardt's winnings of $1 million smashed Gordon's record Winston Cup race winner's purse of $613,000 for winning the 1994 Brickyard 400.

The next week Gordon bounced back at Rockingham, coming from well behind to win the Goodwrench 400. The No. 24

Chevrolet Monte Carlo was so loose that Gordon fell as far back as 31st before fighting back to win his 30th race.

"I think everybody out there got to see us get sideways today because they were all passing me at the beginning," Gordon said. "This is unbelievable. I thought this day might be a disaster. I got out of the car in victory lane and said, 'What am I doing here? I feel like I am in a dream and I haven't woken up yet.'"

And it's a dream that started out as a nightmare.

At Bristol in March a rapid-fire pit stop by his Rainbow Warriors crew helped Gordon gain critical track position and sent him on his way to victory in the Food City 500—his fourth straight victory in the track's spring race. Gordon survived two late cautions and various other scrapes as he led the final 63 laps to become the first two-time winner of the season.

At Charlotte in May, The Winston all-star race provided a bizarre twist in its 14th running. Mark Martin scored his first career victory in the event in a Ford that was unquestionably strong, but outclassed, before Gordon's Chevrolet sputtered and died as it went into Turn 1 on the final lap.

"I'm afraid to say it, but we ran out of gas, I think," Gordon said. "It was pretty embarrassing."

Martin passed Bobby Labonte to take second place as they came out of the fourth turn and headed for the white flag. Gordon was ahead by more than a second, though, and appeared to be heading for a second straight win and his third in four years in the event. When Gordon's car slowed, Martin wasn't sure what to think of it. He sailed by, however, for the win.

As the cars came to start the final 10-lap segment, Gordon was leading, but he got started too quickly.

The start was waved off and the cars circled the track under yellow. Had it not been for that extra distance, Gordon's car might have run out of gas on the way to victory lane.

"They got so far ahead that I couldn't have caught them, but they had trouble," Martin said. "It's a tough break for those guys. They deserved to win it, but we'll take it."

Gordon had plenty of gas for qualifying for the Coca-Cola 600 and he had plenty of power in his No. 24 Chevrolet in winning the pole. For the fifth straight year, Gordon started first in Winston Cup racing's longest event. That tied David Pearson's record for consecutive 600 poles, and he also helped ease some of the disappointment his race team felt since The Winston.

"It was hard," crew chief Ray Evernham said of The Winston. "I sat on the back porch a while Saturday night and thought and thought and thought. I beat myself up. It was my fault.

"I'm the crew chief and it was my deal. When you're the man in charge, you can make up excuses. You can look at this and look at that, but that's a bunch of bull.

"The bottom line is . . . that pit area and that race car is my responsibility."

The STREAK

The Rainbow Warriors dominated the Winston Cup Series like few ever have, especially in NASCAR's modern era.

From June 28 at the Sears Point road course to September 9, 1998 at Darlington, the Rainbow Warriors dominated the Winston Cup Series like few ever have, especially in NASCAR's modern era. Gordon won seven of nine races during the stretch, and finished third at New Hampshire and fifth at Bristol. Both road course events, another Brickyard 400 at Indianapolis, and the Southern 500 at Darlington for the fourth straight time were also among the victories.

As if that wasn't enough to convince the doubters, Gordon won three of the last four races of the year including the season-ending NAPA 500 at Atlanta to register his 13th victory of the year.

That tied Richard Petty for the modern NASCAR record of most wins in a season. Gordon also tied the Winston Cup record for consecutive victories with four and

became the first driver in NASCAR history to win as many as 10 races for three years in a row. He won the No Bull $5 million bonus from R.J. Reynolds for the second straight time with his victory at Darlington.

After clinching the title at Rockingham—with one race left on the schedule—Gordon was asked if he thought there might come a day when he could become bored with dominating his sport the way he had over the past four seasons.

"I just wish I could trade places with you guys for just one day," Gordon said, causing a whole room full of volunteers to raise their hands. When the laughter died, Gordon explained what he meant.

"I say that because if it doesn't look challenging from up here, then I really do wish that you could trade places," he said. "Today was a very challenging race for all the drivers. The challenge never stopped

until the checkered flag waved, and it is like that every weekend.

"I have never gone into a race thinking this is easy. Not at all. I guarantee you anybody who ever thinks that is going to get a rude awakening. . . . Just being out there is challenging to me. Every year offers more competition, it gets tougher and tougher."

1998 Winston Cup Standings (Top 10)

1. Jeff Gordon	5,328
2. Mark Martin	4,964
3. Dale Jarrett	4,619
4. Rusty Wallace	4,501
5. Jeff Burton	4,415
6. Bobby Labonte	4,180
7. Jeremy Mayfield	4,157
8. Dale Earnhardt	3,928
9. Terry Labonte	3,901
10. Bobby Hamilton	3,786

Gordon won the 1999 Daytona 500 to open defense of his title and won six more races during the year, including both road course races again and back-to-back victories at Martinsville and Charlotte in October. Dale Jarrett had finished second to Gordon in '97 and third in '98 but broke through in '99 to win the championship.

The season finale seemed to sum up Gordon's year. In 1998 at Atlanta Motor Speedway, he wrapped up his third Winston Cup championship in four seasons by winning the NAPA 500 to tie Richard Petty's modern-era record of 13 victories in a season.

In 1999, Gordon's No. 24 Chevrolet went out with a blown engine after 181 laps, giving him a 38th-place finish and leaving him sixth in the points standings.

"I'm looking forward to the off-season to get this team back on

track," Gordon said after going out of a race early for the seventh time in the season.

Gordon still won more races than any other driver and scored his final two wins after Ray Evernham left as his crew chief to start his own team with Dodge backing.

After those wins at Martinsville and Charlotte, Gordon finished no better than 10th in the season's final five races. Five members of his pit crew also decided to leave for Jarrett's team in 2000.

"We've got to make a lot of adjustments over the off-season because we lost our pit crew and Ray and a couple of other guys," Gordon said. "We weren't really prepared for this at the end of the season. If you're not perfect, you're not going to be able to win races."

In 2000, Gordon fell to ninth in the standings as Bobby Labonte won his first championship. Gordon won at Talladega, Sears Point, and Richmond.

Before the 2000 season had begun, Robbie Loomis was hired to take over as crew chief for Gordon, who stepped up to take on more of a leadership role with his team. On top of that, Chevrolet changed to a new model of its Monte Carlo heading into the 2000 campaign, and all three teams at Hendrick Motorsports struggled to find the sweet spot on that new car's setup.

"One of the things that I pride myself on is that I've always been able to adapt myself to situations, new types of race cars and new types of setups," Gordon said. "As quickly as things turned last year to the different type of setups we were running, I don't feel like I

adapted quickly enough to them. I didn't get the confidence level that I needed.

"I always have to push myself to new limits," he added. "You have to drive the car differently than you used to have to drive it. I've got to make sure that I don't get set in old ways."

Those old ways had been good to Gordon entering 2001, bringing him 52 Winston Cup victories, three championships, and victories in NASCAR's premier event, the Daytona 500, in 1997 and 1999.

"I think that the success that this team and I had over the past years is what allowed us to get through a year like that," Gordon said. "When you win a lot of races and you've won championships, if you have a bad year you know what it took to get to the top."

A FRIEND
losing

The 2001 Daytona 500 saw a lethal crash for seven-time champion Dale Earnhardt and cast a huge shadow over the sport. Gordon won the pole the following week and paid tribute to his rival and friend. He wore a Dale Earnhardt cap for interviews after taking his 34th career pole position.

"He was somebody I respected greatly and I learned a lot from him—more than he ever imagined," Gordon said. "That's why I put this No. 3 hat on and let everybody know we're thinking of Dale. I want to dedicate this to him. It's a great opportunity to let everyone know how much I respected him and how much we're going to miss him."

Attention turned to the void Earnhardt's death would leave in NASCAR, but Gordon refused to get swept up in the talk of who would be "the next Dale Earnhardt."

Replacing Earnhardt, he said, shouldn't even be a part of the equation.

"Why does the sport have to move on without the memory of Dale Earnhardt?" Gordon said. "I think that's always going to be a presence, forever."

Gordon regained the form of his championship seasons and won the third race of the year at Las Vegas, then opened June with victories at Dover and Michigan. He led 381 of 400 laps in the former and the latter gave Rick Hendrick his 100th win as a team owner.

In October Gordon dodged wrecks, penalties, and other calamities that cost his rivals dearly to win the inaugural Winston Cup race at Kansas Speedway, the 20th track on which Gordon had gone to victory lane.

At age 30, a fourth Winston Cup championship looked inevitable. Gordon was already one of seven

> *"He was somebody I respected greatly and I learned a lot from him—more than he ever imagined," said Gordon.*

drivers with at least three titles, and on average the other six didn't win their first titles until age 33. Richard Petty and David Pearson were 34 when they won No. 3.

It took Petty 15 years to win four titles, Dale Earnhardt 12.

Gordon dodged the inevitable questions about whether he could break Petty and Earnhardt's record of seven titles.

"It's hard for me to look ahead and think that's a possibility," Gordon said. "What I always do is just focus on the next one, the next race, and the next championship and that's it."

Gordon didn't win another race in the 2001 season after Kansas, but he still secured his fourth title.

Dale Earnhardt had won his sixth and seventh titles in Gordon's first two full seasons of Winston Cup competition, 1993 and '94, while Gordon watched and learned.

"He was so good at knowing when to win and when to bring that thing home to get the points," Gordon said. "There are some guys who just have a special knack for knowing how to get the most out of a car.

"He knew where he could shine and where he just had to get all that he could. He never gave up, never. That guy, it didn't matter whether his car was way off or if he was laps down, he never stopped driving the wheels off of that thing. Every position, every point means something.

"He wanted to be that eight-time Winston Cup champion and he got seven of them because he knew what he was doing. Winning races is great, but there's nothing better than winning championships."

2001 Points Finish

1. Jeff Gordon	5,112
2. Tony Stewart	4,763
3. Sterling Marlin	4,741
4. Ricky Rudd	4,706
5. Dale Jarrett	4,612
6. Bobby Labonte	4,561
7. Rusty Wallace	4,481
8. Dale Earnhardt Jr.	4,460
9. Kevin Harvick	4,406
10. Jeff Burton	4,394

The FUTURE

Gordon's success rate in NASCAR's top series almost defies anyone's belief. His 58 victories lead all active drivers, and he got his first win at 22, much younger than Bobby Labonte (31), Dale Jarrett (34), Rusty Wallace (29), and Bill Elliott (28).

"A lot of the guys didn't get to Winston Cup until later than I did," Gordon said. "I was able to get with a top organization from the start and that allowed me to be successful at a lot younger age."

If Gordon keeps his pace and wins four more titles in the next nine seasons, he'll get a record eighth championship in 2010 with his 40th birthday still a season away. But he's not sure he or anybody else can reach that feat.

"They're wearing us out," he said. "The schedule is so intense, and it's not just 36 races. It's that plus everything that comes along

with having a $15-million-per-year sponsor.

These guys are paying a lot of money and they expect to get something in return for their investment, and I expect them to.

"When you're a champion, opportunities come along that are hard to turn down ...Those things will shorten how long you're going to race."

Or have to race, he says.

"If I were to stop today, I would have to change my lifestyle. That shouldn't be the determining factor, but if there comes a day when you're not having fun and the desire is not there and you ask if you can give up all of the other stuff, I certainly could.

"As long as I am healthy and competitive and the desire is there I am going to keep racing," Gordon says. "I don't put an age limit on it, but if any one of those things goes

> *If Gordon keeps his pace and wins four more titles in the next nine seasons, he'll get a record eighth championship in 2010 with his 40th birthday still a season away.*

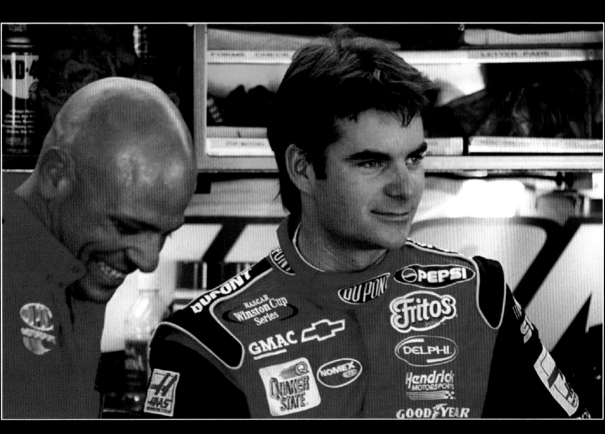

away it could stop me sooner."

Gordon's blip—the departure of crew chief Ray Evernham and an ensuing upheaval and retooling of his team at Hendrick Motorsports—didn't come until after his third title, and it lasted only two seasons. So far, Gordon has avoided major injuries that are always a risk for a Winston Cup driver, and his emotional batteries seem recharged by his new leadership role in the team.

He has a lifetime contract with Hendrick Motorsports and is part owner in the No. 48 team with young phenom Jimmie Johnson as driver. In 2002, Johnson became the third rookie ever to win a pole for the Daytona 500.

"I admire Jeff so much," said Tony Stewart, who finished second in the 2001 standings and looms as a possible rival to Gordon's future success. "He gets it right every time. No matter the situation, it seems like he handles it exactly the right way."

Like a champion.